MASTERCLASS

Brazilian Jiu Jitsu

Ultimate Armlocks

By
Ricardo Arrivabene

P.O. Box 491788, Los Angeles, CA 90049
www.empirebooks.net

Disclaimer
Please note that the author and publisher of this book are NOT RESPONSIBLE in any manner whatsoever for any injury that may result from practicing the techniques and/or following the instructions given within. Since the physical activities described herein may be too strenuous in nature for some readers to engage in safely, it is essential that a physician be consulted prior to training.

Published in 2007 by Empire Books.
Copyright © 2007 by Empire Books.

All rights reserved. No part of this publication may be reproduced or utilized in any form or by any means, electronic or mechanical, including photocopying, recording, or by any information storage and retrieval system, without prior written permission from Empire Books.

Library of Congress Cataloging-in-Publication Data

ISBN-13: 978-1-933901-30-5
ISBN-10: 1-933901-30-6

Arrivabene, Ricardo, 1966-
  Masterclass Brazilian jiu jitsu : ultimate armlocks/ by Ricardo Arrivabene --1st ed.
      p. cm.
  Includes index.
  ISBN 1-933901-30-6 (pbk. : alk. paper)
 1. Jiu-jitsu--Brazil. I. Title. II. Title: Brazilian jiu jitsu. III. Title: Jiu jitsu.
  GV1114.S274 2006
  796.815'2--dc22
                                         2006009376

Empire Books
P.O. Box 491788
Los Angeles, CA 90049
(818) 767-7900

First edition
07 06 05 04 03 02 01 00 99 98 97 1 3 5 7 9 10 8 6 4 2
Printed in the United States of America.

Interior Photography: Jason Alan
Interior & Cover Design: Mario M. Rodriguez, MMR Design Solutions

Dedication

To my family – for their support and love through the hard times.

Acknowledgement

I thank all of my instructors for giving me the understanding and knowledge to undertake all the martial arts projects I've done during my life. I also thank all of my friends whose constant encouragement motivated me to keep going and keep growing.

To my brother Eduardo, for helping me to illustrate all the techniques.

You all have my enduring thanks,

Ricardo Arrivabene

ABOUT THE AUTHOR

RICARDO ARRIVABENE

Ricardo Arrivabene is a professional Brazilian Jiu Jitsu instructor and acclaimed champion who began his martial arts training in Brazil. His extensive knowledge of Brazilian Jiu Jitsu allowed him to win many championships. Mr. Arrivabene has shared many hours of extensive training with the top names of Brazilian Jiu Jitsu and is one of the most sought-after instructors in the world.

He is passionate about the importance of the art of Brazilian Jiu Jitsu in the world of martial arts, but yet at the same time patient and understanding to those who practice it. His performance in competition is flawless and his skills second to none. Years of practice and training have forged this icon of Brazilian Jiu Jitsu into a living embodiment of fighting spirit, "the fundamental idea of the traditional teachings of Jiu Jitsu is the development of effective fighting or self-defense skills. Without such idea there is no Jiu Jitsu, and the mental aspect or attitude is paramount in this."

After many years dedicated to the practice of the art, Master Arrivabene keeps walking the same path, immersing himself in the training and development of his beloved art, with no changes in his mind about what Jiu Jitsu is or is not.

TABLE OF CONTENTS

INTRODUCTION .... page ix

From the Mount
Page 1

From the Guard
Page 8

From the Side Mount
Page 46

From the Side Control
Page 60

From the Back
Page 82

From the Side Back
Page 88

From the Standing Position
Page 96

CONCLUSION 108

INTRODUCTION

It is almost impossible to trace the exact origins of the techniques known today as armlocks. Different cultures, and the fighting methods they originated, use the exact same technical movements to control the opponent's arms. From the Greeks to the Indians, including the Chinese and the Japanese arts, the application of a locking technique in the opponent's arm is one of the fundamental methods of submitting an adversary.

By simple description, an armlock is a single or double joint lock that hyperextends, hyperflexes, or hyperrotates the elbow joint and/or shoulder joint. An armlock that hyperextends the elbow joint is called an armbar, and an armlock that hyperflexes or hyperrotates the shoulder joint is referred to as a shoulder lock. Depending on a person's joint flexibility, armlocks that hyperrotate the shoulder joint also can hyperrotate the elbow joint, and vice versa. The pressure is applied directly against the elbow when the arm is straight, and indirectly when it is bent.

Regardless of the style and method you practice, there are only a limited number of ways an arm can be manipulated in order to apply an armlock. When doing it, you'll be applying force in the direction opposite to the natural movement of the arm. Therefore, it is very important to understand the basic and fundamental principles that make these armlock techniques effective. All armlock techniques use the principle of pull/push. This is a fundamental principle associated to all joint-locks, regardless of the style or method. You'll find yourself pulling in one direction and pushing in another at the same time to create the lock. Once you understand those

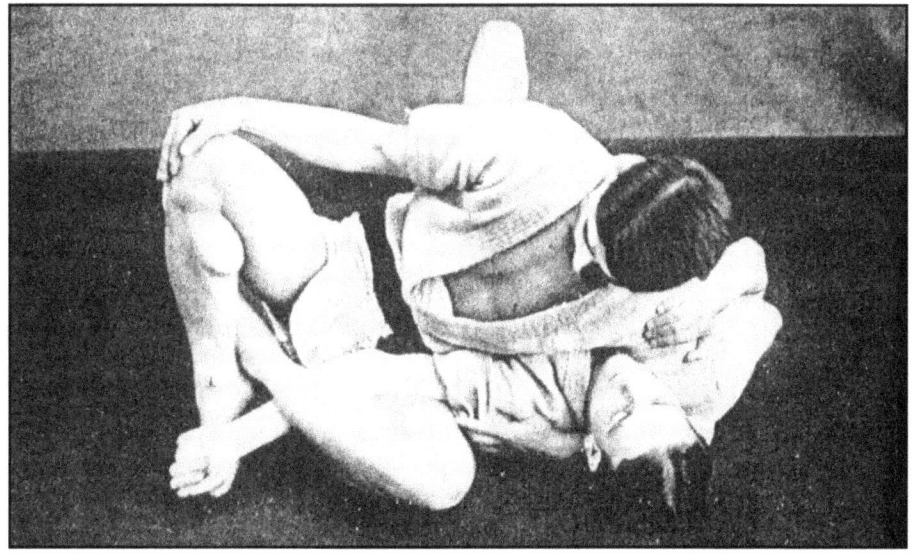

Introduction

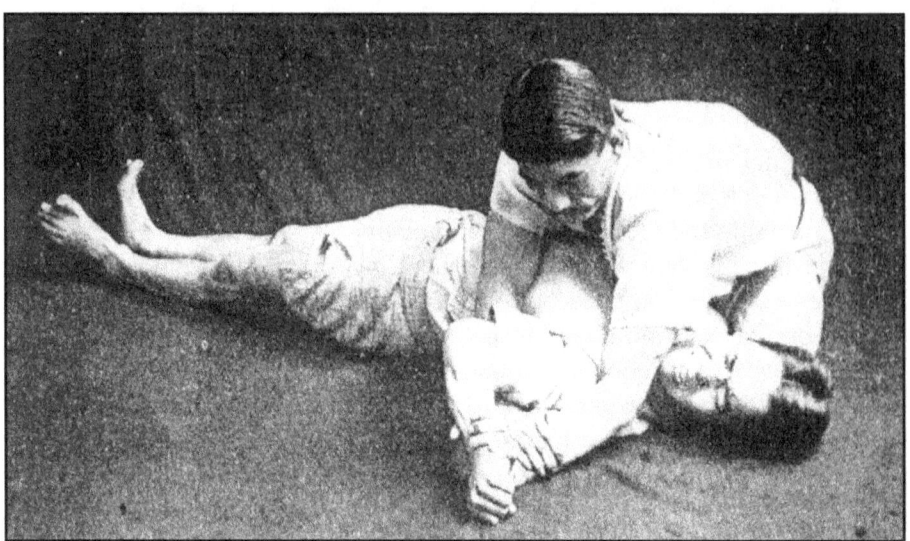

principles, new possibilities will be open for you regarding how to apply the same armlock from very different positions. You will see that the principles and concepts that make the armlocks are still the same, but the approach to their application varies as the circumstances demand. A principle can be applied to many situations, but a technique will be limited to a certain environments and circumstances. It is important to develop an effective use of full-body leverage in order to initiate and secure a lock on the arm. In this book, we'll be dealing mainly with the application of armlocks from the perspective of Brazilian Jiu Jitsu. Armlocks usually are more easily performed from a grappling position on the ground, such as the guard, the mount, side control, etc. They are more difficult to apply when both fighters are standing.

This book will teach you the basic and fundamental armlocks in the art of Brazilian Jiu Jitsu, but you will not learn by reading and trying them once. You know the strenuous practice that champions undergo; yet, to become a good Jiu Jitsu practitioner, you need only half their time and practice, and not even one-tenth of their energy. But you must practice consistently!

The Structure of the Arm

When studying the different techniques of armlocks, we need a fundamental understanding of where in the arm we can apply the pressure. All armlock techniques fall into the application of pressure in three areas: shoulder, elbow, and wrist.

Shoulder: Because of its structure, the shoulder joint has the greatest range of motion of all the joints, but this characteristic also makes it a very easy joint to pop up when the pressure is applied. Because it is formed in a ball-and-socket fashion, it doesn't need to break to get damaged. It is a very unstable joint and any strange movement can dislocate it, damaging all the tendons and ligaments holding the joint. Many Brazilian Jiu Jitsu competitors have dislocated their shoulders when attempting to escape from an armlock.

Elbow: This is the part of the arm that is mostly attacked when trying to get the opponent in an armlock. Because of its structure, the elbow joint can't move further back when the arm is completely straight. Any further pressure will cause the elbow to break. The elbow is composed of three separate joints (radius, ulna and humerus bones) and supported by four ligaments. If an elbow is broken due to an armlock, all these ligaments will be seriously damaged.

Wrist: Due to its size, the wrist is used in combination with other areas when applying an armlock. It is more difficult to control and, although it can be easily damaged, it is mainly used as leverage for other locking techniques to the elbow and shoulder. Some wristlocks are applied in Brazilian Jiu Jitsu, but because of the nature and structure of the techniques, it is easy for the opponent to escape before we can finalize the lock.

Types of Armlocks

ARMBAR

A straight armbar is, by definition, a joint lock that hyperextends the elbow joint. It is applied by placing the opponent's extended arm at the elbow over a fulcrum such as a leg or hip, and controlling the opponent's body while leveraging the arm over the fulcrum. The technique has several variations and can be applied from many different positions, such as the side control, the guard, the mount, etc. In a basic straight armbar, the attacker grabs the wrist of the targeted arm of the opponent, holding and securing it by squeezing it between the thighs of the attacker. The attacker's legs end up across the opponent's chest, with the arm held between the thighs and the elbow pointing against the thigh or hips. By holding the opponent's wrist to the

Helio Soneca.

INTRODUCTION

Grandmaster Carlos Gracie, Sr.

attacker's chest, and with the thumb pointing up, the attacker can extend the opponent's arm and hyperextend the opponent's elbow, creating pressure in the elbow joint. The attacker can further increase the pressure by arching his or her hips against the elbow. The necessary pressure is obtained by lifting the knee upward but keeping the feet in contact with the mat to prevent the opponent from freeing his arm. Hold the opponent's captured arm firmly between your thighs.

Pointers:

1. Keep constant pressure on your opponent's arm as you lift it. This prevents the arm from bending and allows you to stretch the arm as you roll backward.
2. Keep the lowered buttock as close as possible to your opponent's shoulder joint.
3. The outside leg serves both to control the opponent's head and to scissor his arm tightly.

Counter-Technique:

It is necessary that you escape from this technique before your opponent starts applying pressure. Right when the opponent starts to lean on his back, twist your hand a little, bend your elbow, and pull your hand down with force. Turn your body to the side, because if you stay lying on your back, you will not be able to withdraw your arm.

You can also try to escape by slipping out under the attacker's controlling leg by using the hand to push/pull the opponent's leg out of position, then sitting up into the lock.

BENT-ARMLOCK

A bent-armlock or figure-four armlock involves holding the forearm and using it to twist the upper arm laterally. It usually is considered a shoulder lock since the primary pressure often is on the shoulder. A shoulder lock is a technique that hyperflexes or hyperrotates the shoulder joint. A shoulder lock is applied by forcing the arm beyond its normal range of shoulder-wise movement, which can be done in many different ways. Typically, the body is prevented from moving by using either a leg or a pinning hold, and the arm is then pulled, pushed, or twisted in the other direction. It can be applied from many different positions, and is the most common shoulder lock used as a submission hold in Brazilian Jiu Jitsu competition. This technique has several variations and the word "reverse" sometimes is added to signify medial rotation, as in reverse bent-armlock, which in this case indicates lateral rotation.

Pointers:
1. Make sure you control the opponent's body properly.
2. Completely control the opponent's shoulder.

Counter-Technique:

A general method of escape is to turn around quickly in the direction in which your arm is being twisted. Turn your head and shoulder to that side so that it resists the opponent's action and pull your arm out of the lock.

AMERICANA

This technique is applied only from the mount or side mount, since it needs support from the ground to be fully effective. The opponent's arm is pinned to the ground so that it is bent at the elbow, with the palm upwards. The wrist is grabbed with the opposite hand, and the arm on the same side

Grandmaster Helio Gracie.

INTRODUCTION

Paulo Guillobel.

is put under the opponents arm, grabbing the opponent's wrist using a figure-four hold. While keeping the opponent's hand pinned to the ground, begin sliding the pinned arm down and lifting the elbow upwards. Use the opponent's wrist as you would use a brush when painting. The movement will put a great deal of pressure on the opponent's shoulder.

Pointers:

1. Make sure that the palm of the opponent's hand is facing upward.
2. Completely control the opponent's shoulder.
3. Use his wrist to transmit the pressure to his elbow.

Counter-Technique:

A general method of escape is to turn around quickly in the direction in which your arm is being twisted. Turn your head and shoulder to that side so that it resists the opponent's action and pull your arm out of the lock.

KIMURA

Also known as a "chicken wing" in Wrestling circles. The application is similar to the Americana, except that it is reversed. It needs some space behind the opponent to be effective, and can be applied from the side mount or guard. In this case, the opponent's wrist is grabbed with the hand on the same side, and the opposite arm is put on the back side of the opponent's arm and again grabbing the attacker's wrist and forming a figure-four. By controlling the opponent's body and pulling the arm away from the attacker, pressure is put on the shoulder joint. This technique was named after the legendary judoka Masahiko Kimura, who defeated Helio Gracie with the use of this armlock.

Pointers

1. Apply it quickly with a simple twisting motion.
2. Push strongly toward the opponent's back.

Counter-Technique:

The best method of escape is to turn around quickly in the direction in which your arm is being twisted and pull your arm out of the lock. Timing

Marcio Feitosa.

is everything when you try to escape from a "kimura."

OMOPLATA

The "omoplata" is a commonly featured shoulder lock in Brazilian Jiu Jitsu. The locking mechanism is very similar to the Kimura, but instead of using a figure-four, it is applied using a leg. The omoplata can be applied from the guard when you are in a defensive position. By controlling the opponent's body and pushing the arm perpendicularly away from the opponent's back, pressure can be put on the opponent's shoulder to apply the technique. It is a very effective technique but, because of its nature, it is more difficult than other armlocks to apply successfully.

Pointers:

1. Make sure to tightly control the opponent's arm with your leg.
2. Maintain perfect balance at all times by using your supporting hand on the ground and the other grabbing the opponent's belt.

Counter-Technique:

If you find yourself in a situation where your opponent's feet are placed in position and you cannot pull your arm out, push his thigh with your free hand; this will take his foot off your left thigh. Then, roll your body to the side, move upward and pull your arm out.

FLYING ARMBAR

INTRODUCTION

Luis Heredia.

The flying armbar is a version of the basic crossed armbar that is performed from a stand-up position. It is typically applied when the opponent has a collar tie. By tightly holding the opponent's neck and arm, the attacker puts one of his or her shins against the opponent's midsection and leans up on the opponent; at the same time, the attacker swings the leg on the same side as the opponent's collar tie over the opponent's head, into the typical armbar position. The flying armbar is considered to be one of the most spectacular joint locks in competitions, but it is uncommon because of the risk of losing position and getting into a disadvantageous situation.

Pointers:

1. Maintain a tight grip on the collar to support your bodyweight.
2. Bring your hips close and tight to the opponent's trapped arm.

Counter-Technique:

Simply withdraw the elbow of the trapped arm down and close to your own body as you suddenly turn your body to the side where the opponent is jumping. Even if the opponent goes up and jumps over your shoulder, he won't be able to get the armlock.

TIPS

In all aspects of the different armlock techniques, certain points should be observed carefully:

- The whole body always must be comfortably relaxed. Use the mechanical advantage of placing yourself in a stronger position.

- The weight of the attacker's body should be on the mat and not on you. This will give you leverage to apply the lock.

- Once the armlock has been applied, the Brazilian Jiu Jitsu fighter must maintain the same relative position between himself and the opponent. He must therefore follow every move the adversary makes, insuring that his presently-secured position is not jeopardized. To fully control your opponent's body movements, you must make at least one of his arms weak and incapable of changing positions.

- When applying an armlock, make sure you position yourself in a way that gives you the greatest leverage to apply the pressure. Turning and lifting some body parts will increase the pressure in the application of the technique.

- In order to achieve the above principle, it is essential that the Jiu Jitsu fighter's posture on the mat be poised and flexible.

- Never persist with a control position when the arms and legs have been partially compromised. Change to another type of guard or break away. Reposition yourself as soon as you realize that you do not have complete control of your opponent's movements. Remember, this control will open the doors for the final submission technique.

- Always be watching for the opportunity to apply an armlock, because in the course of your opponent's struggles, he just may give you the opening you require.

- Always use correct posture because this is the key to transferring your bodyweight effectively into the armlock.

- Principles always are more important than the techniques they produce.

- The armlock techniques must be applied quickly and surely, in order to control the movement of the opponent's arm with confidence.

- Be careful when training. When applied improperly or with excessive force, armlocks can cause muscle, tendon, and ligament damage, even dislocation, or bone fractures.

ARMLOCKS

FROM THE MOUNT

1. Arrivabene is mounting his opponent and controlling the left arm.

2. Now, he moves his hips to the right and brings his right hand onto the opponent's chest, as he simultaneously opens the mount position by lifting his left knee off the ground.

Technique 1

3. He sits down on the opponent's left side without letting the arm go...

4. ...and leans back to apply a straight armlock.

ARMLOCKS
FROM THE MOUNT

1. Arrivabene is mounting the opponent and, with his right hand, grabs the opponent's left sleeve and pulls it.

2. Then, he crossed the opponent's left arm across the body...

3. ...as he simultaneously brings his left leg to the outside...

TECHNIQUE 2

4. ...and passes it under the opponent's right shoulder.

5. Without losing control of the opponent's arms,

6. He leans forward and applies a straight armlock to the opponent's right arm.

Armlocks

FROM THE MOUNT

1. Arrivabene controls the opponent from the mount position and makes sure the arms are trapped.

2. He moves to the left and moves to turn his position without losing control of the arms.

3. Then, Ricardo passes his left arm under the opponent's right arm...

4. ...and leans forward to grab the opponent's left leg with his right arm.

TECHNIQUE 3

5. Now, he moves his right leg close to the opponent's left shoulder...

6. ...and begins to roll forward...

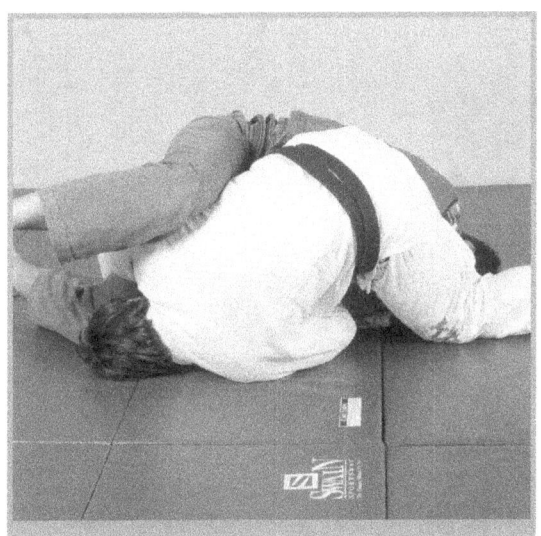

7. ...without letting go either the arm or the leg.

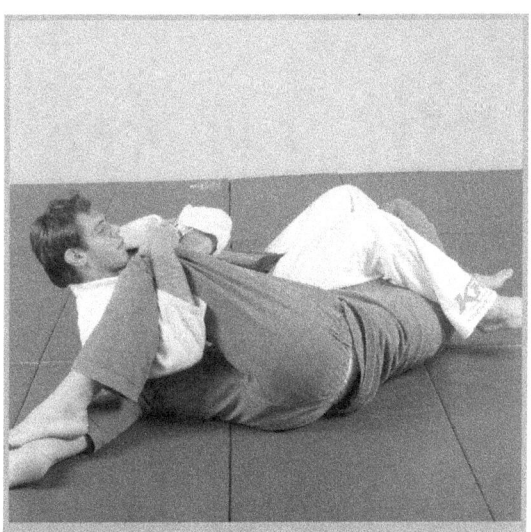

8. From the side of the opponent, Ricardo applies a straight armlock without releasing the grip on the opponent's left leg.

ULTIMATE ARMLOCKS

ARMLOCKS

FROM THE MOUNT

1. Ricardo is mounting his opponent and controlling the opponent's left arm.

2. With his right hand, Arrivabene reaches for the opponent's right lapel...

3. ...and secures the grip by placing his left hand on the opponent's left shoulder.

TECHNIQUE 4

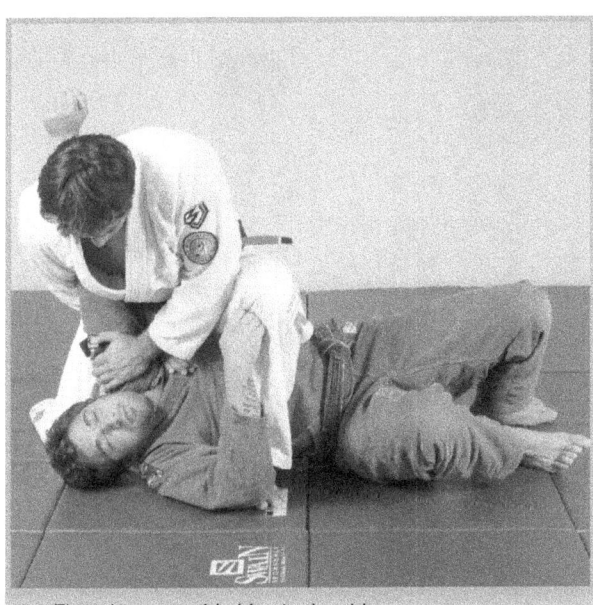

4. Then, he moves his hips to the side...

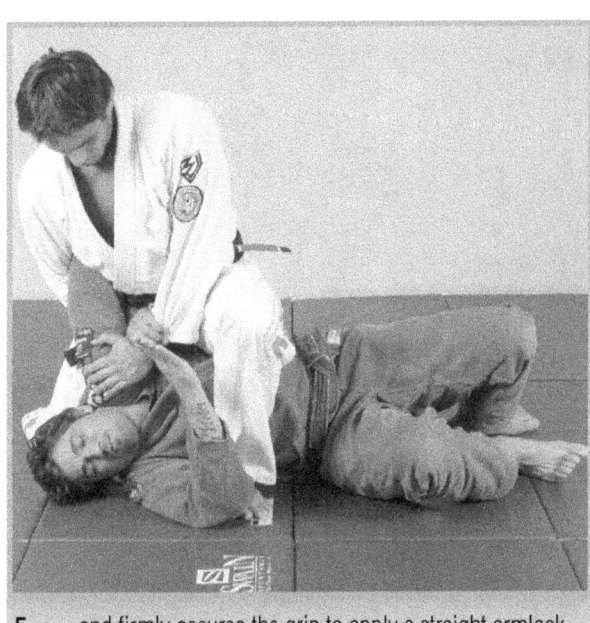

5. ...and firmly secures the grip to apply a straight armlock with pressure in the elbow.

ARMLOCKS

FROM THE GUARD

1. Arrivabene has the opponent inside of his guard.

2. He uses his left hand to grab the opponent's right sleeve...

3. ...and then grabs the full arm with his right hand.

4. Now, Ricardo uses his left hand to grab the left side of the opponent's collar.

TECHNIQUE 5

5. Ricardo brings his left leg up while maintaining control of the arms...

6. ...and passes his right leg along the opponent's left side of the back until he reaches the armpit.

7. Then, he brings his left leg to the front and over the opponent's head and applies a straight armlock.

Armlocks

FROM THE GUARD

1. Ricardo controls the opponent from the closed guard.

2. Supporting his body on the two-hand grip, Ricardo brings his feet up and places them on the opponent's thighs, as he simultaneously pulls both sleeves close to his chest.

3. Then, he brings his right leg up and places it on top of the opponent's left shoulder...

Technique 6

4. …and does the same things with his left leg.

5. From that position, he brings his hips upward and applies pressure to deliver a double-straight armlock.

ARMLOCKS
FROM THE GUARD

1. Arrivabene controls the opponent inside of his closed guard.

2. Without opening the legs, Ricardo moves his hips to the left as he simultaneously controls the opponent's right arm.

TECHNIQUE 7

3. He spins his body around, opens the left leg and...

4. ...pushes with both legs down and, after bringing the left leg over the opponent's head, applies a straight armlock.

ARMLOCKS

FROM THE GUARD

1. Ricardo has the opponent under control inside his closed guard but now he controls the opponent's left arm by grabbing it with his right hand.

2. Now, he opens the guard and move his hips to the right side as he simultaneously brings the opponent's arm close to his right shoulder.

Technique 8

3. He slides his body to the side and brings his right leg on top of the opponent's back to add pressure as he applies a straight armbar.

Armlocks

FROM THE GUARD

1. Ricardo shows the same technique, but from the other angle. He passes his left hand under the opponent's right arm...

2. ...and pulls it to the inside as he simultaneously grabs his left hand with his own right hand for better support.

Technique 9

3. Then, he pulls in the arm and moves his left leg over the opponent's right shoulder to apply the final armbar.

ARMLOCKS
FROM THE GUARD

1. Ricardo has the opponent controlled inside of his closed guard.

2. He grabs the opponent's left sleeve and pulls it all the way up to his head to unbalance the opponent's posture.

3. Then, he passes his right arm around the opponent's left arm...

4. ...and grabs the opposite lapel with the right hand to maintain tight control.

Technique 10

5. Now, he opens the guard…

6. …and pushes the opponent's left shoulder with his left hand…

7. …to apply the final armbar.

ARMLOCKS

FROM THE GUARD

1. Arrivabene controls the opponent using the spider guard.

2. He pulls the opponent's left sleeve to the side and brings his right leg inside and all the way up to the opponent's neck, as he controls the other side with his left foot on the opponent's right hip.

Technique 11

3. Then, he passes the right shin and places it in front of the opponent's neck as he simultaneously pulls the right sleeve with his left hand.

4. Now, Ricardo brings his left leg in front and around the opponent's head and releases the grip on the left sleeve to apply the final armlock.

ARMLOCKS

FROM THE GUARD

1. Ricardo has the opponent controlled inside of his closed guard.

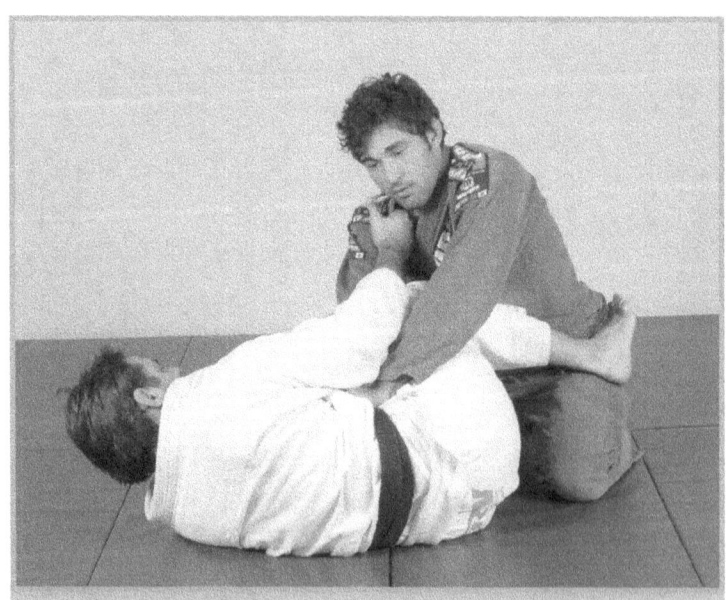

2. ...and pulls hard to bring the opponent's head down with the help of his right hand.

TECHNIQUE 12

3. Ricardo opens the guard and brings his right leg up as he simultaneously pulls hard with his left hand…

4. …to bring his left leg over the opponent's head to apply the straight armlock.

Armlocks

FROM THE GUARD

1. Ricardo has his opponent inside of his closed guard.

2. Then, he uses his right hand to push the opponent's head to the side...

3. ...but he makes sure that the opponent's left arm is under control.

4. Now, Ricardo brings his right leg up...

Technique 13

5. ...and reaches with his left hand...

6. ...to grabs his own right ankle.

7. With the opponent's left arm trapped between Ricardo's leg and body...

8. ...Arrivabene begins to turn to the side and adds pressure to the position...

(CONTINUED ON NEXT PAGE)

Armlocks

(CONTINUED FROM PREVIOUS PAGE)

9. ...until the opponent's face touches the ground.

10. Now, Ricardo reaches with his left hand...

11. ...and grabs the opponent's left leg.

12. Then, he pulls hard to the side as he rolls his own body to the right...

Technique 13

13. ...to bring the opponent on his back...

14. ...without losing control of the opponent's left arm.

15. From that position, Ricardo applies a straight armlock.

ARMLOCKS

FROM THE GUARD

1. Ricardo has his opponent inside of his guard. The opponent is standing up to pass the guard.

2. Arrivabene uses his left hand to grab the opponent's right sleeve...

3. ...and passes his right hand behind the opponent's left ankle.

4. Then, he pulls hard with his left hand and moves his body slightly to the right...

Technique 14

5. ...so he can bring the opponent's body down and reach out and grab the left side of the collar.

6. Now, with the opponent's head down, Ricardo brings his left leg up...

7. ...and places it around the opponent's head to apply a straight armlock.

ARMLOCKS

FROM THE GUARD

1. Arrivabene has his opponent inside of his guard. The opponent is standing up to pass the guard. Ricardo uses his left hand to grab the opponent's right sleeve.

2. Now, he passes his right hand in front of both of the opponent's legs...

3. ...as he secures the grip of the opponent's left sleeve with his left hand.

4. With the opponent's head down, Ricardo brings his left leg up and places it around the opponent's head.

Technique 15

5. From this position, Ricardo pushes down and brings the opponent to the ground...

6. ...where he maintains control of the opponent's right leg...

7. ...and simultaneously applies a straight armlock.

ARMLOCKS

FROM THE GUARD

1. The opponent is standing, waiting to pass Ricardo's open guard.

2. Ricardo reaches with his right hand and grabs the opponent's left sleeve.

3. Then, he pulls hard to bring the opponent's body down.

Technique 16

4. With his left hand, Ricardo reaches out and grabs his opponent's right ankle…

5. …as he simultaneously brings his right foot down and puts the "hook" behind the opponent's left leg.

(CONTINUED ON NEXT PAGE)

Armlocks

(CONTINUED FROM PREVIOUS PAGE)

6. Then, he brings his left foot down and places his left knee behind the opponent's right leg.

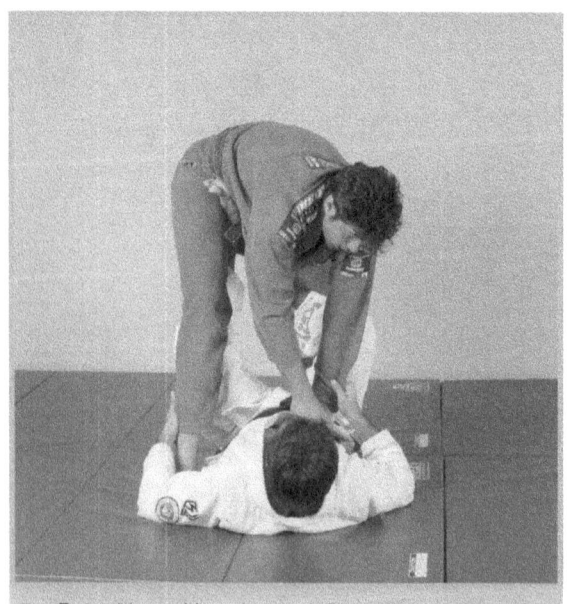

7. From this position of control, Ricardo unbalances the opponent's posture...

8. ...and moves his hips to the right to allow space to bring his right leg to the outside...

Technique 16

9. ...so he can sweep the opponent to the ground...

10. ...and apply the final straight armlock.

ARMLOCKS

FROM THE GUARD

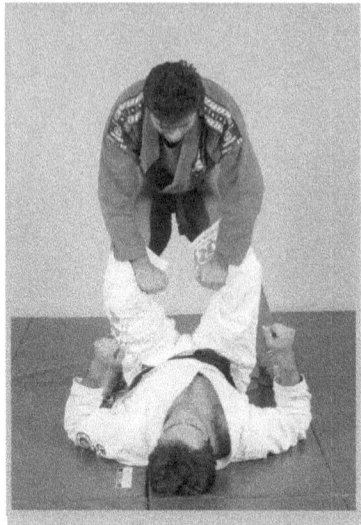

1. The opponent is standing, waiting to pass Ricardo's open guard.

2. Ricardo reaches with both hands and grabs both of the opponent's sleeves.

3. Then, he pulls and brings the opponent's body down as he simultaneously slides his hips forward.

4. Now, Arrivabene controls the action with both feet placed on the opponent's hips...

5. ...and pushes hard with the right leg to make the opponent's body turn to the right in the air...

Technique 17

6. ...as he simultaneously opens his left leg to allow the body...

7. ...to fall onto the left side.

8. Then, Ricardo pulls the opponent's arm hard with both hands...

9. ...and applies a straight armlock.

ARMLOCKS

FROM THE GUARD

1. The opponent is standing, waiting to pass Ricardo's open guard.

2. Ricardo reaches with his both hands and grabs the opponent's right sleeve.

3. Then, he pulls hard to bring the opponent's body closer...

Technique 18

4. ...and he reaches with his left hand to grab the opponent's right ankle.

5. Without losing control of the opponent's left arm, Ricardo opens his right leg...

6. ...and begins to pass it in front of the opponent's head...

(CONTINUED ON NEXT PAGE)

Armlocks

(CONTINUED FROM PREVIOUS PAGE)

7. ...to place it over the opponent's right triceps.

8. Then, he brings the right foot and hooks it under the arm, securing it on the opponent's right side of the chest.

9. By putting downward pressure with his right leg...

Technique 18

10. …and by pulling the opponent's left arm with his right hand…

11. …Ricardo applies a straight armbar.

Armlocks

FROM THE GUARD

1. The opponent is standing, waiting to pass Ricardo's open guard.

2. Ricardo reaches with his both hands and grabs the opponent's right sleeve.

3. Then, he pulls hard to bring the opponent's body closer...

4. ...and he reaches with his left hand to grab the opponent's right ankle.

TECHNIQUE 19

5. Without losing control of the opponent's left arm, Ricardo opens his right leg…

6. …and begins to pass it in front of the opponent's head…

7. …to place it over the opponent's right triceps.

8. Then, he brings the right foot and hooks it under the arm, securing in on the opponent's right side of the chest.

(CONTINUED ON NEXT PAGE)

Armlocks

(CONTINUED FROM PREVIOUS PAGE)

9. Now Ricardo pushes hard and unbalances the opponent's position...

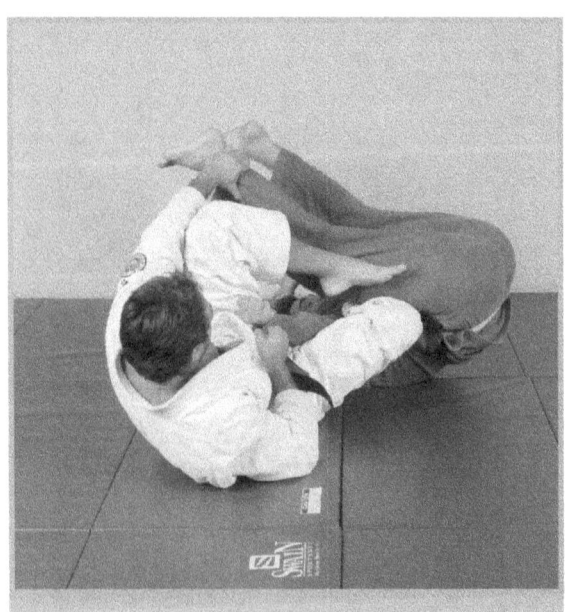

10. ...bringing him down to the ground...

11. ...without releasing either the grip on the opponent's right ankle...

Technique 19

12. ....or the grip on the right sleeve.

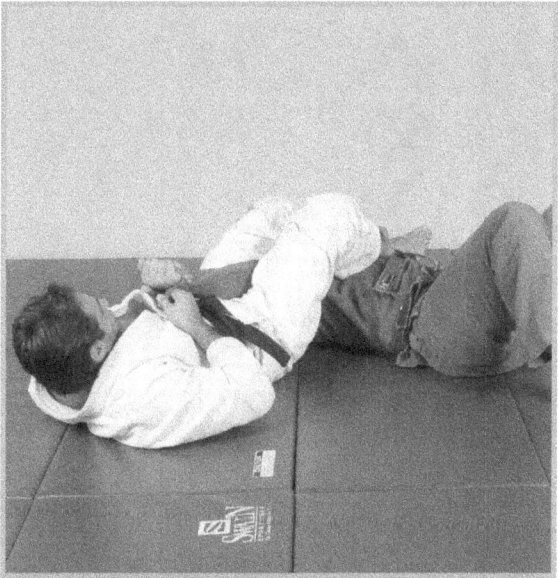
13. Then, Arrivabene pulls hard from the sleeve to adjust the opponent's arm position...

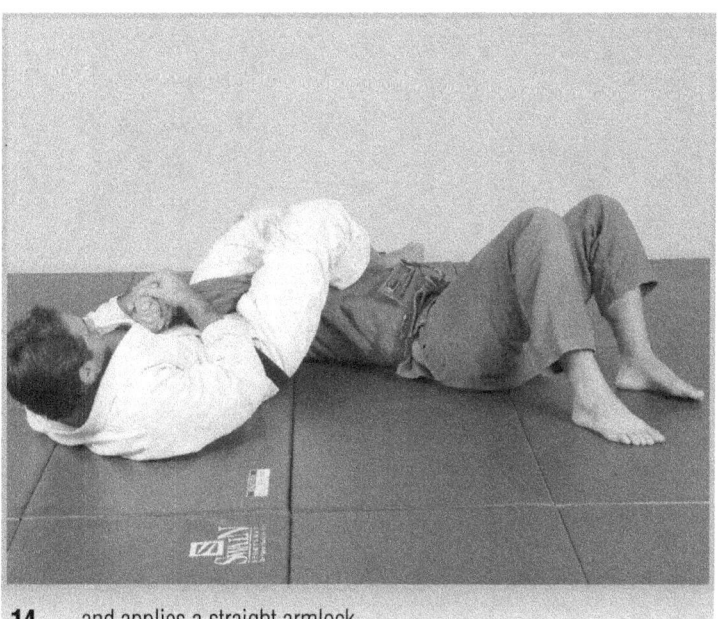
14. ...and applies a straight armlock.

ARMLOCKS

FROM THE SIDE MOUNT

1. Arrivabene controls his opponent from the side mount.

2. The opponent is trying to push Ricard's left knee...

3. ...to which Ricardo reacts by bringing his left hand...

4. ...and grabbing the opponent's right hand from below.

Technique 20

5. Then, he wraps the opponent's arm under his armpit...

6. ...moves his hips to the right side...

7. ...passes his left foot over the opponent's head...

8. ...and applies a straight armlock.

ARMLOCKS

FROM THE SIDE MOUNT

1. Ricardo controls the opponent from the side mount with the knee on the stomach.

2. He grabs the opponent's right sleeve and pulls up hard.

3. Then, Ricardo uses his right hand to control the upper part of the opponent's arm.

Technique 21

4. By putting his left hand on the opponent's chest, Arrivabene creates a base…

5. …to spin around and apply a final straight armlock.

Armlocks

FROM THE SIDE MOUNT

1. Arrivabene controls the opponent from the side mount with one knee on the stomach.

2. Using his right hand, Ricardo controls the opponent's left side of the collar and...

3. ...simultaneously underhooks the opponent's right arm with his left hand.

Technique 22

4. He begins to spin around the opponent's head to pass to the other side.

5. Now, he bends his right leg and...

6. ...sits down to apply a final straight armlock.

ARMLOCKS

FROM THE SIDE MOUNT

1. Arrivabene controls the opponent from the side mount with the knee on the stomach.

2. Using his right hand, Ricardo controls the opponent's left side of the collar and simultaneously underhooks the opponent's right arm with his left hand.

Technique 23

3. But this time, instead of spinning around, he maintains his position and brings the opponent's arm close to his body.

4. Then, he brings his right knee and places it on top of the opponent's head as he simultaneously applies a straight armbar.

ARMLOCKS

FROM THE SIDE MOUNT

1. Ricardo controls the opponent's left side of the collar with his right hand to base his side mount position.

2. He underhooks the opponent's right arm with his left hand.

3. Now, Ricardo brings the opponent's arm close to his body...

TECHNIQUE 24

4. ...and passes his right leg over the opponent's head.

5. Without letting the right arm go, Ricardo sits down and applies a straight armbar to the opponent's right arm.

ARMLOCKS

FROM THE SIDE CONTROL

1. Ricardo controls the opponent from the scarf hold position.

2. He passes his right arm under the opponent's head and grabs the inside of his right thigh to achieve better control of the opponent's body.

3. Then, he brings his left hand and grabs the opponent's right wrist to straighten the arm.

Technique 26

4. Now, Arrivabene brings his left leg and places it over the opponent's right arm...

5. ...to push down and apply a straight armlock

ARMLOCKS

FROM THE SIDE CONTROL

1. Ricardo controls the opponent from the side position.

2. Using his left hand, he controls the opponent's right arm...

3. ...and brings it all the way down to the ground.

TECHNIQUE 27

4. Now, he passes his right hand under the opponent's right elbow and grabs his own left wrist to create leverage.

5. Moving his right knee closer to the opponent's head, Ricardo adds pressure to the position…

6. …before he fully brings the knee over the head and applies a straight armlock.

ARMLOCKS

FROM THE SIDE CONTROL

1. From the side, Arrivabene controls the opponent, who is trying to escape.

2. Ricardo uses his left hand to create a base and support...

3. ...to pass his left leg over the opponent's head.

Technique 28

4. Then, he grabs the opponent's right arm with his left hand and brings his right leg over the opponent's body as he simultaneously maintains his hips very close to the opponent's right shoulder.

5. Now, he sits on the ground and applies a straight armlock.

ARMLOCKS

FROM THE SIDE CONTROL

1. From the scarf hold, Ricardo controls the opponent.

2. He brings his right knee close to the opponent and passes it over the opponent's right arm.

3. Without losing control of the arm, he passes the leg to the other side and grabs the opponent's right sleeve.

4. Now, he pulls the right arm up...

Technique 29

5. ...and begins to move to the other side by passing his right leg in front of the opponent's head.

5. ...and begins to move to the other side by passing his right leg in front of the opponent's head.

ARMLOCKS

FROM THE SIDE CONTROL

1. Ricardo has the opponent under control, but this time he is pinning the opponent's left arm close to his head.

2. Now, he passes his right hand across the opponent's chest and grabs his own left lapel to trap the opponent's left arm..

3. Without losing control of the arm, Arrivabene brings his hips forward and

4. ...passes his right left over the opponent's head...

Technique 30

5. to sit down.

6. Now, he brings his left hand into play and with both hands, controls the opponent's left arm.

7. He tilts his hip up and applies pressure for a straight armlock.

Armlocks

FROM THE SIDE CONTROL

1. Arrivabene controls the opponent from the side. The opponent has his right arm over Ricardo's left shoulder.

2. Ricardo passes his right arm over the opponent's head and moves the head to the other side of the opponent's right arm.

3. Then, he brings his right arm and traps the opponent's right arm close to his right collarbone.

Technique 31

4. Now, Ricardo circles to the right and controls the opponent in the north & south position.r

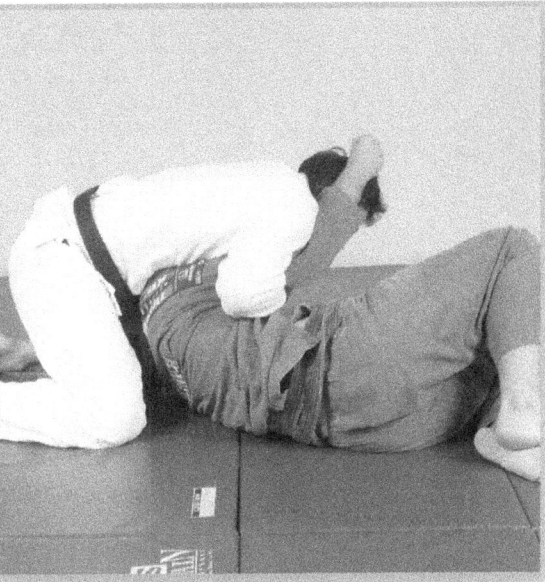

5. Without releasing the the trapped arm…

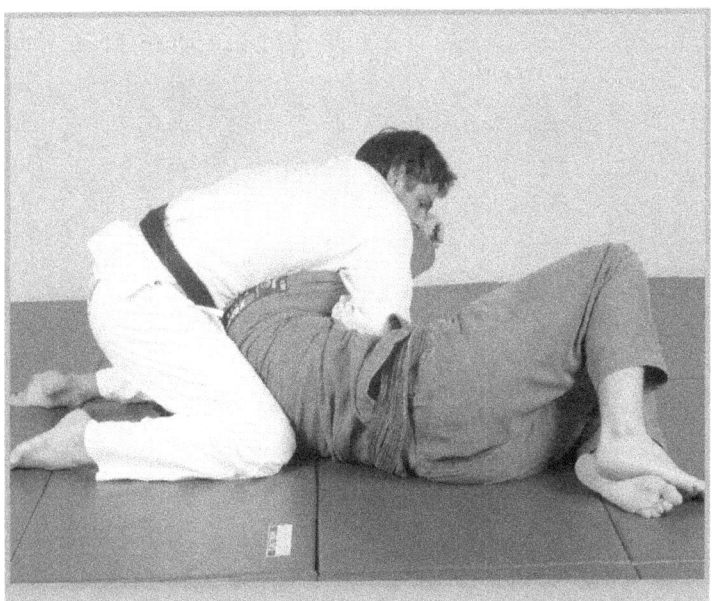

6. …he keeps his body close to the opponent's back by bringing his right knee up.

(CONTINUED ON NEXT PAGE)

Armlocks

(CONTINUED FROM PREVIOUS PAGE)

7. Then, Ricardo lift his left leg and passes over the opponent's head.

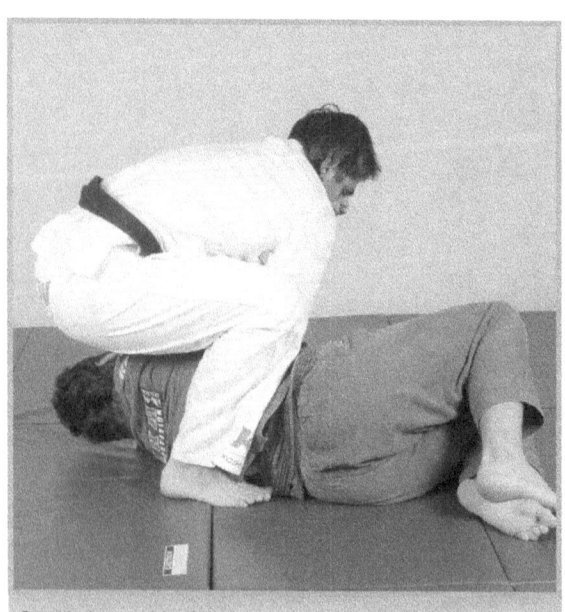

8. He leaves his right knee up and...

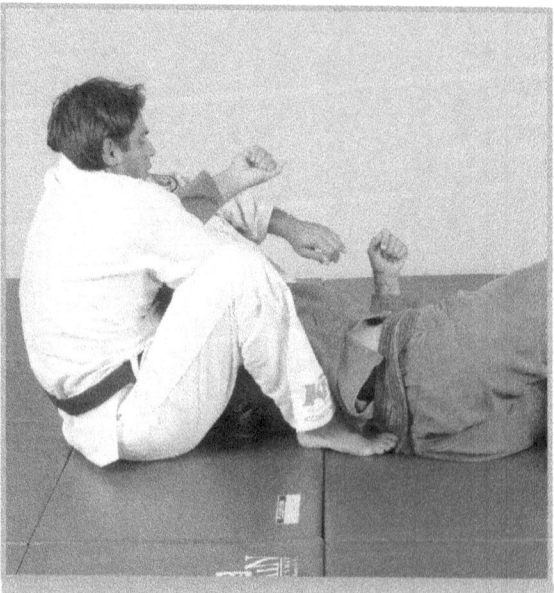

9. ...without releasing the trapped arm...

Technique 31

10. ...he sits down and...

11. ...applies a straight armlock.

ARMLOCKS

FROM THE SIDE CONTROL

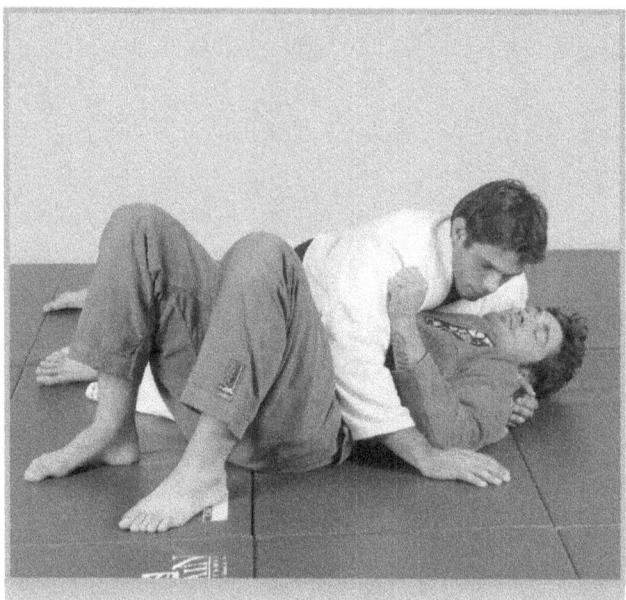

1. Arrivabene controls his opponent from the side position.

2. Ricardo brings his right hand and traps the opponent's left arm...

3. ...by grabbing the left side of his collar.

TECHNIQUE 32

4. Without releasing the grip, Ricardo begins to circle around toward the opponent's head…

5. …and brings his right knee up.

(CONTINUED ON NEXT PAGE)

Armlocks

(CONTINUED FROM PREVIOUS PAGE)

6. Then, he uses his left hand to grab the opponent's left leg...

7. ...as he simultaneously brings his left leg and places it on the opponent's left side of the body.

8. Once he has a tight grip on both the arm and the leg, Ricardo sits down on the ground...

Technique 32

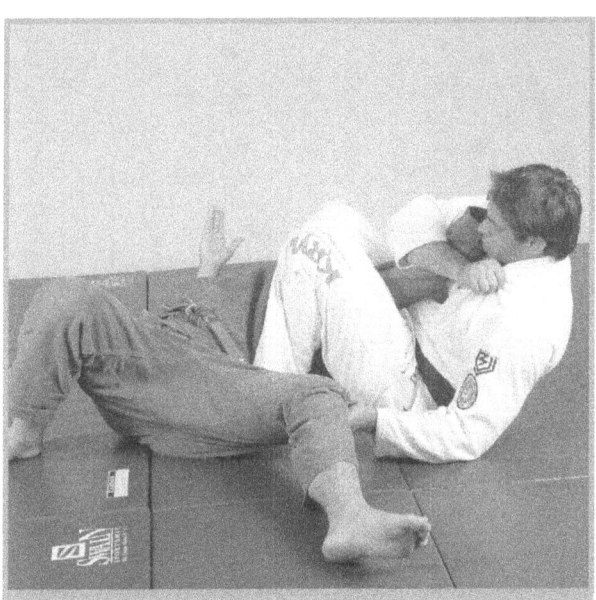

9. ... pulls back with the left hand to bring close the opponent's left leg ...

10. ...and applies a straight armlock.

Armlocks

FROM THE SIDE CONTROL

1. Arrivabene controls the opponent from the side position but the opponent has his right leg up to prevent Ricardo from mounting him.

2. Ricardo brings his right hand and places it behind the opponent's right knee.

3. Then, he reaches out and grabs the opponent's right wrist without losing control of the opponent's collar with his left hand.

TECHNIQUE 33

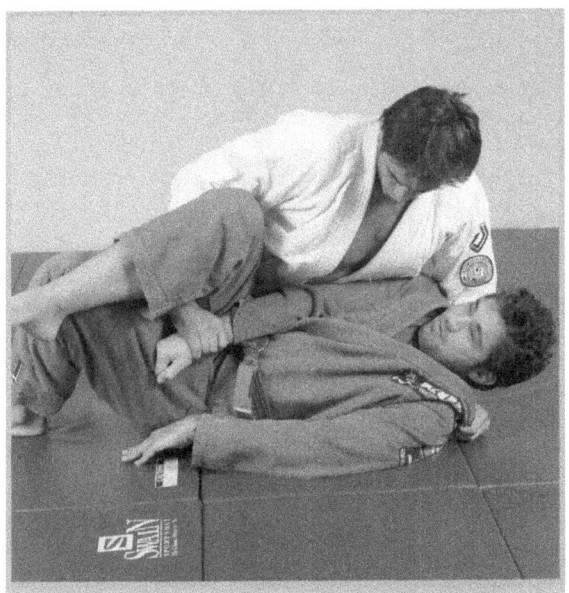

4. Now, Arrivabene brings his trunk up and begins to pull the opponent's right wrist back.

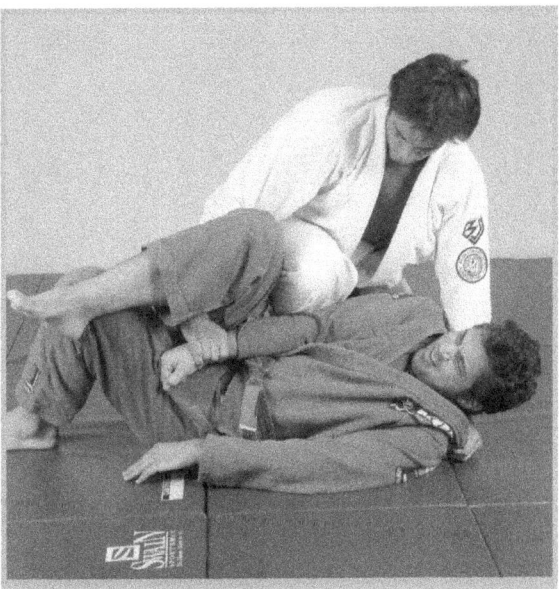

5. Then, he puts his right knee up and places it right behind the opponent's elbow joint.

6. Simultaneously, he pulls from the wrist and pushes away with his right knee, applying a straight armbar.

ARMLOCKS

FROM THE SIDE CONTROL

1. Arrivabene controls the opponent but the opponent has his right leg up to prevent Ricardo from mounting him.

2. Ricardo brings his right hand and places it behind the opponent's right knee.

3. Then, he reaches out and grabs the opponent's right wrist without losing control of the opponent's collar with his left hand.

Technique 34

4. Now, Arrivabene begins to pull the opponent's right wrist back, but this time he twists his left hand around the opponent's neck and brings it to the front.

5. Then, he puts his right knee up and places it right behind the opponent's elbow joint.

6. Simultaneously, he pulls from the wrist and pushes away with his right knee, applying a straight armbar and a choke with his left hand.

Armlocks

FROM THE BACK

1. Ricardo is controlling his opponent from the back.

2. He secures the "hooks" and begins to move his body to the left...

3. ...so he can pass his left arm under the opponent's left armpit and reach the right side of the lapel.

4. Then, Arrivabene uses his right hand to push the opponent's head to the right...

Technique 35

5. ...to create space so he can pass his right leg...

6. ...over the opponent's head...

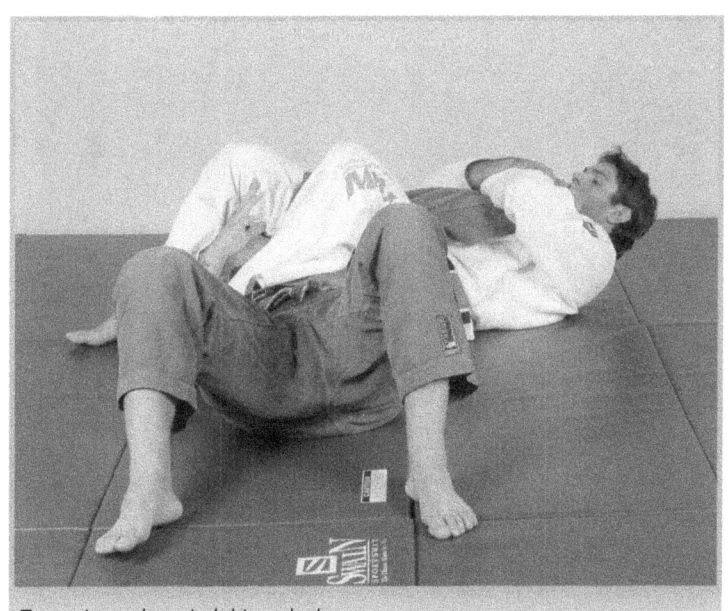

7. ...to apply a straight armlock.

Armlocks

FROM THE BACK

1. Ricardo is controlling his opponent from the back with the "hooks" and have his two hands grabbing the opponent's collar.

2. Now, he uses his right hand to grab the opponent's left wrist...

3. ...and with his own left hand, Ricardo grabs his own right wrist.

4. Then, he passes his right arm to the other side of the opponent's head...

Technique 36

5. ...to create space so he can pass his right leg...

6. ...over the opponent's head...

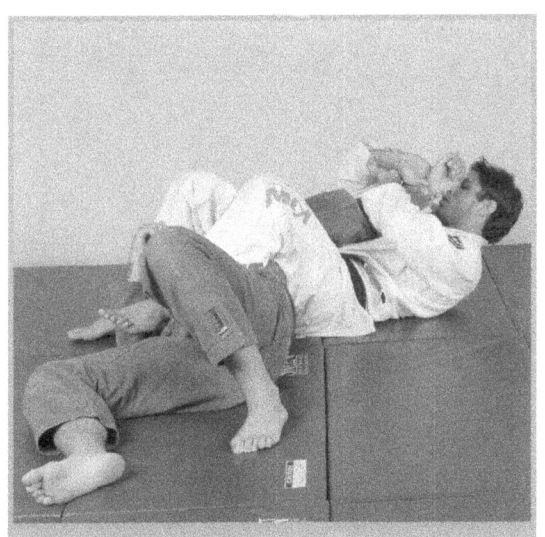

7. ...to pull the arm all the way back...

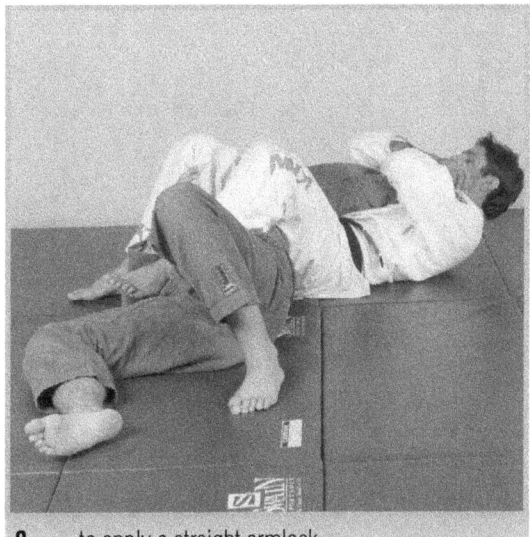

8. ...to apply a straight armlock.

Armlocks
FROM THE BACK

1. Ricardo is controlling his opponent from the back.

2. He secures the "hooks" and simultaneously grabs the opponent's left collar with his right hand.

3. Now, he begins to move his body to the left…

4. …and pulls hard with his right hand as he lets his body touch the ground.

Technique 37

5. Without losing control of the grip and without passing his right leg over the opponent's head...

6. ...he pulls the opponent's left arm back...

7. ...and applies a straight armlock.

Armlocks

FROM THE SIDE BACK

1. From the side, Arrivabene controls the opponent who is on his fours.

2. Ricardo brings his right knee inside and behind the opponent's left arm as he simultaneously puts pressure by leaning forward with his chest.

3. Then, he passes his left foot forward and...

TECHNIQUE 25

4. ...hooks the opponent's left arm...

5. ...between his legs for a better control.

(CONTINUED ON NEXT PAGE)

Armlocks

(CONTINUED FROM PREVIOUS PAGE)

6. Now, Arrivabene passes his right leg over the opponent's back...

7. ...and begins to roll forward...

8. ...without losing control of the grips and the hooks.

Technique 25

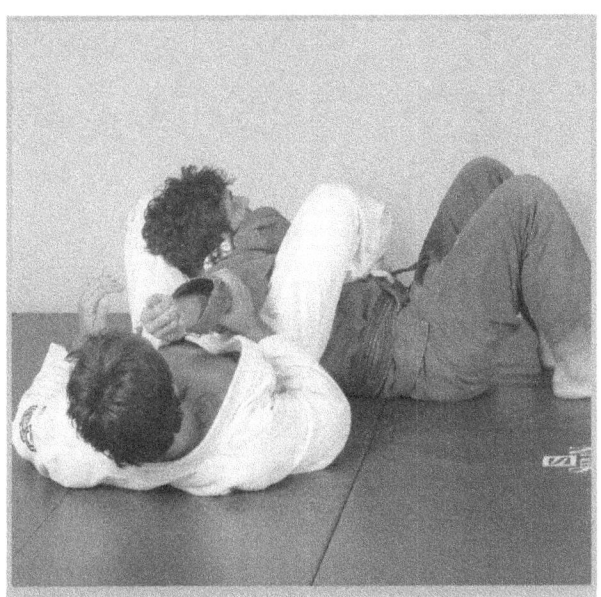

9. Once on the ground, he maintains a tight control on the grip…

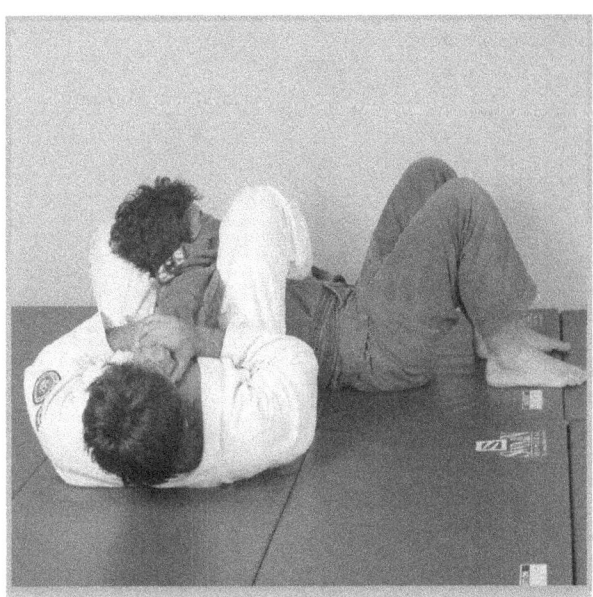

10. …and applies a straight armlock.

ARMLOCKS

FROM THE SIDE BACK

1. Ricardo's opponent is on his fours.

2. Ricardo, with his left hand, grabs the inside of the collar and with the right hand the opponent's belt.

3. Then, he brings his right leg over the opponent's back...

4. ...and begins to let his body roll forward...

Technique 38

5. ...to the other side of the opponent's position...

6. ...without letting the grips in the collar and the belt go.

7. Once the roll has been completed, Ricardo opens up his left leg,

8. passes it over the opponent's head and applies a straight armlock.

ARMLOCKS
FROM THE SIDE BACK

1. Ricardo's opponent is on his fours.

2. Ricardo with his right hand grabs the inside of the collar and with the left hand the opponent's belt as simultaneously brings his left knee behind the opponent's right arm.

3. Then, he passes his right foot forward and...

4. ...hooks the opponent's right arm...

Technique 39

5. ...between his legs for a better control,

6. Then, he leans forward and begins to put pressure to...

7. ...apply a straight armbar.

ARMLOCKS

FROM THE SIDE BACK

1. From the side, Arrivabene controls the opponent who is on his fours. With his left hand, Ricardo grabs the inside of the collar, and with his right hand, the opponent's belt.

2. Now, Arrivabene passes his right leg over the opponent's back...

3. ...and passes his left arm under the opponent's left armpit.

TECHNIQUE 40

4. Then, he brings his left knee close to the opponent's head...

5. ...and begins to roll forward...

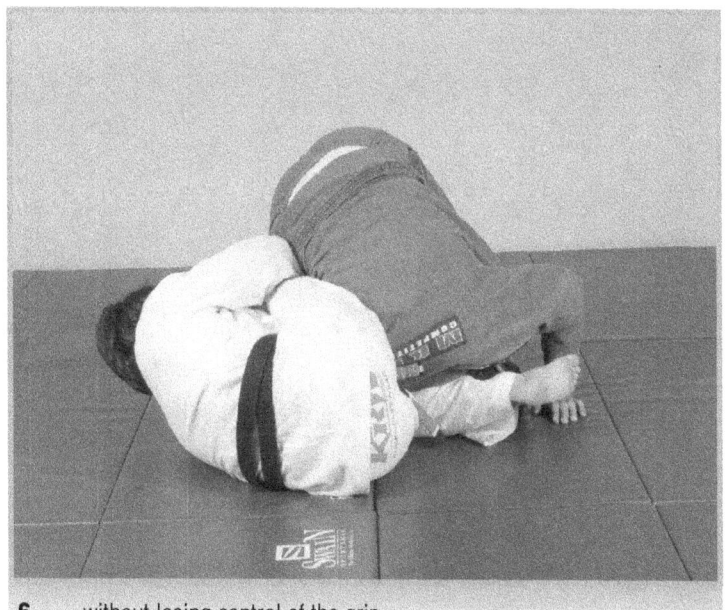

6. ...without losing control of the grip.

(CONTINUED ON NEXT PAGE)

Armlocks

(CONTINUED FROM PREVIOUS PAGE)

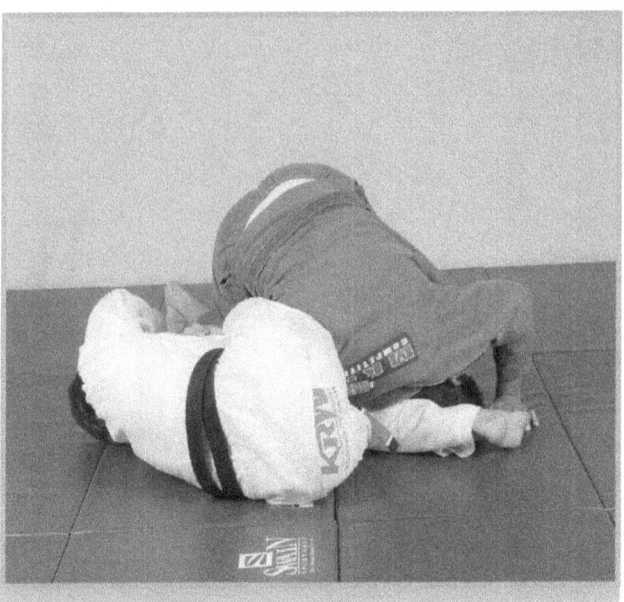

7. With his right hand, Ricardo reaches and grabs the opponent's right leg...

8. ...and pulls hard to the side...

9. ...to bring the opponent on his back.

TECHNIQUE 40

10. Now, Ricardo pulls hard to tighten up the grips…

11. …and let the leg go for a better control in the straight armlock.

Armlocks

FROM THE STANDING POSITION

1. Ricardo is facing his opponent in a standing position.

2. Then, he brings his right leg up...

3. ...places it on the opponent's left thigh...

Technique 41

4. ...and lets his body fall onto the ground without losing control of the grips on right sleeve and left lapel.

5. Once on the ground, Arrivabene passes his right hand behind the opponent's left leg...

(CONTINUED ON NEXT PAGE)

Armlocks

(CONTINUED FROM PREVIOUS PAGE)

6. ...as he simultaneously brings his left leg around and places it over the opponent's head.

7. Then, he pushes forward and brings the opponent onto the ground...

8. ...while he maintains full control of the right leg.

TECHNIQUE 41

9 Without losing the grip on the arm...

10. ...Ricardo begins to slide back...

11. ...and applies a final straight armlock.

ARMLOCKS

FROM THE STANDING POSITION

1. Ricardo is facing his opponent in a standing position.

2. He brings his right arm under the opponent's right armpit...

3. ...and moves his feet to take a position...

4. ...to prepare the hip throw.

Technique 42

5. By bringing the hips down...

6. ...he begins to unbalance the opponent forward...

7. ...without releasing the grip of the right arm.

8. Then, Ricardo brings his body down...

(CONTINUED ON NEXT PAGE)

Armlocks

(CONTINUED FROM PREVIOUS PAGE)

9. ...and throws the opponent...

10. ...onto the ground.

11. Now, Arrivabene brings his right knee and puts it on the opponent's chest.

Technique 42

12. He passes his left leg over the opponent's head...

13. ...and sits down on the ground to apply a straight armlock.

ARMLOCKS
FROM THE STANDING POSITION

1. Ricardo is facing his opponent in a standing position.

2. The opponent moves in with his right leg to try a throw.

3. He successfully throws Ricardo down...

Technique 43

4 ...and begins the offensive on the ground.

5. Ricardo maintains a tight grip on the opponent's right sleeve and collar and begins to open his left leg...

6. ...so he can pass it around the neck.

(CONTINUED ON NEXT PAGE)

ARMLOCKS

(CONTINUED FROM PREVIOUS PAGE)

7. Once the leg has been secured around the opponent's neck...

8. ...Ricardo pushes forward and down...

9. ...to bring the opponent onto the ground...

Technique 43

10 ...without releasing the grips.

11. Then, he lets the left leg go and brings his right hand to help control the opponent's right arm...

12. ...to apply the final straight armlock.

CONCLUSION

CONCLUSION

Remember that a sound knowledge of armlocks is a very effective weapon for any practitioner of Brazilian Jiu Jitsu. When training at the school, forget the competition and aim solely to be efficient, even if it means performing techniques and movements in which you are not skillful. Jiu Jitsu's legacy is always to emerge victorious from a fight. The Jiu Jitsu practitioner's goal is to emerge from battle the victor. To endure the journey, one must find the enjoyment and humor within the process. Like art, Jiu Jitsu is a painting with many strokes that in the end will unveil a masterpiece. Have fun with your training!

The Publishers

www.ingramcontent.com/pod-product-compliance
Lightning Source LLC
Chambersburg PA
CBHW081351080526
44588CB00016B/2456